TABLET FRAGMENTS

TABLET FRAGMENTS

TAMAR RUBIN

Clarise Foster, Editor

Signature
EDITIONS

Cover design by Doowah Design.
Cover art by Nava Yefet Rubin: "Unravelling Fear, Stepping into Hope," watercolour on paper, 2017.
Photo of Tamar Rubin by Leif Norman.

This book was printed on Ancient Forest Friendly paper.
Printed and bound in Canada by Marquis Book Printing.

We acknowledge the support of The Canada Council for the Arts and the Manitoba Arts Council for our publishing program.

Library and Archives Canada Cataloguing in Publication

Title: Tablet fragments / Tamar Rubin ; Clarise Foster, editor.
Names: Rubin, Tamar, 1986- author. | Foster, Clarise, 1955- editor.
Description: Poems.
Identifiers: Canadiana 20200184423 | ISBN 9781773240657 (softcover)
Classification: LCC PS8635.U297 T33 2020 | DDC C811/.6—dc23

Signature Editions
P.O. Box 206, RPO Corydon, Winnipeg, Manitoba, R3M 3S7
www.signature-editions.com

TO MY BOYS

Contents

PROLOGUE

The first time Moses ascended Mount Sinai to receive the Divine revelation, he came down, after forty days and forty nights, bearing two stone tablets, inscribed with the words of the Law.

As he descended, he saw the Children of Israel dancing – confused, abandoned, ecstatic – worshipping a Golden Calf.

Moses – confused, abandoned, angry – threw down the stone tablets, upon which were written not just the words of the Commandments, but the entire revelation of justice, history and wisdom.

The tablets shattered into a thousand fragments.

Moses ascended Mount Sinai a second time, negotiated with God for a second chance, and came down, after a further forty days and forty nights, bearing two new inscribed stone tablets, which were placed inside the wood Ark of the Covenant.

The Levites collected all the broken fragments of the first set of stone tablets and placed them inside the Ark of the Covenant, alongside the two new unbroken tablets. And the Children of Israel carried both sets of tablets – the whole and the shattered – on their journey through the desert.

The Kabbala teaches that the Ark is a symbol of the human heart. And that brokenness – of the stamped-on glass, when the bride and groom stand under the wedding canopy; of the created world, when the Divine light shatters its earthly vessels – is an essential aspect of the wholeness of life.

And Rabbi Menachem Mendel of Kotzk says: "There is nothing more whole than a broken heart."

DOMESTIC
DISHARMONY

We have gone astray; **תָּעִינוּ**
We have led others astray; **תִּעְתַּעְנוּ**
We have turned away **סַרְנוּ**

HOME ARCHEOLOGY

Within this house, words
for things we own: spatula,
womb chair, driveway. Terms I know

look good on display.

Museum or mausoleum. Inside, we
decorate ravenously, sustain succulents,
lampshades, blandly
say nothing.

You make the supper, Moroccan
pomegranate, fall off the bone
beef. We eat

straight out of that orange tagine
from our wedding, and its skeletal
memory.

We thrash out dishes, laundry, utility
bills. But I don't say anything, really.
Yesterday was my turn to talk

with the therapist. Dig, she said.
I try to play

archaeologist, excavate awful
relics inside me:

spyglass, school desk, a first print
of Tolstoy.

But my mouth is all cushions,
and carpets – words, and material clutter
strangle me.

RENOVATION POEM 570 A-3

Silence, but for the talk of renovation.

I name the colours of the skyline as we drive:
peach cloud, citrus, yellow flash –

Each word a pleasing chip of how our lives might go

together, with a brand-new kitchen.

GREY

Neither of us names the tone

in this room. I forgot we chose this
particular paint.

We argued a lot, I cried
over tiles, paid

for a very quiet garburator. Our taciturn dishwasher,

half open, emits traces
of dinner, the moisture left

hanging. It is no one's turn
to carry these vessels. No one

speaks, but a glass
could smash, storm cloud walls

crash down, and drown
the almost burnt out light bulb

in a flash.

STITCHES

With catgut, I hem haws,
socks, slacks, my sternum
threatens to crack. I pierce through panties,
shrink

my husband's gaps.

After work mending patients, I patch things up
at home, try to be a good surgeon, never

butcher dinner. I smile because my grandmother
once said: stitching will make you a good wife.

CULTURE AND SENSITIVITIES

My husband can tackle walled-off chaos, lance
boils, evacuate effectively when needed.
The anarchy of microbes does not faze him.

He tells me an abscess is a healthy body
sequestering infection after failing
rejection. Inflammation organizes –
platelets, fibrin, skin cells like soldiers
guarding their target.

He permeates strongholds, extracts infiltrators
from out-of-place spaces. In a fresh-pressed shirt
clean slacks, requisition

in hand. He is prepared for putrefaction
with containers labelled "culture
and (antibiotic) sensitivity."

He was raised this way,
to face certain complications, turn away from others.

It is unexpected messiness
that gets him:

Milk left out on the counter, months
planned carefully, a bloodstain
on a perfectly good pair of panties.

SALAD EXPERIMENT

I. Here is a recipe for misery:

A spoonful of honey, dripping, a plan
to withhold it.

Do not put your heart into it.

Slice, cut, chop, hack. Massacre
a cucumber.

Forget radishes, the flesh of the thing.
Omit peaches. Expect

peaches. Do not expect
tartness under fuzzy skin.

Make dinner, to be a good wife.
Never make dinner
to prove a point.

II. Balanced eating is difficult.

In winter, we try variations,
withstand

anemic lettuce, a salad-bowl version of failure.

In summer, we drown
in surplus, and nothing

turns out with the taste I expected.

I hate heirloom
tomatoes, the legacy of obsolete

dinners. I need something bloodier –
Give me the knife and I'll try

not to butcher the simplest dressing again.

ARGUMENT, BIBLICAL PROPORTIONS

It's time to talk.
The honeymoon is over.
Missile after missile, I kept telling you

Stop.

I want to love you, but I can't

dismantle your warhead.

I am not scared of conflict. The struggle of Jacob all night till the dawn
is what named him,

Israel. We are both full of fire, and the injury
that fuels it.

But before you incinerate,
think: no one is an angel.

With a mighty hand and an outstretched arm –
be gentle, hold on

to honour, principles. It wasn't anger

that convinced a rock to make water, that planted
a tree in its honour.

Let us cast seeds, a kernel of tenderness, and flowers

might find a bed
between a rock and a pillow.

MIDDLE PAIN

Sometime between the city, and summer at the lake

an egg dropped. I didn't notice

the ache, how quietly we'd stopped
trying.

Now, a rebound pain: remembering

the names we wrote in sand, how perfectly the waves
obliterated them, repeating

hopes, returning shells.

"Middle pain" is the direct translation of the medical term "Mittelschmerz." It refers to mid-menstrual cycle pain caused by ovulation.

COLD START

Cold email, doorbell
      broken, no answer, walking back
into wind instrument
      slapping sharp note against
my throat's hard pit. A violin

      snaps back, twinging speechless
resonance, bone-
      dense cords, a quiet beating
heart plays dumb. Ice follows

      frozen fingers, engine
spits inside.
      Open car, consolation
heat escapes in salty rain, wheels spin
      a game of downhill
skeleton.

MOTHERHOOD/ DAUGHTERHOOD/ GENESIS

And these words, וְהָיוּ הַדְּבָרִים הָאֵלֶּה

which I command you today אֲשֶׁר אָנֹכִי מְצַוְּךָ הַיּוֹם

shall be upon your heart עַל לְבָבֶךָ

and you shall teach them sharply וְשִׁנַּנְתָּם

to your children לְבָנֶיךָ

PERENNIAL

For thirty-one years, my mother tried not to miss her. Every week,
a little water or the trickle of a few ice cubes
dropped

in black earth. Years back, in the muck of Toronto, April,
my grandmother visited from Israel, left
a Christmas cactus

the vast beach of my mother's Mediterranean
mother – oranges, mangoes, brown skin, hot
tempers, a bowl of warm milk for stray cats –
all packed inside this

tiny hammered copper vessel. For fifteen years after
my grandmother's death, this house plant

kept moulting, blooming. Blooming, moulting, against the grain of North
American weather. Sometimes I caught my mother, comfortable

inside unfamiliar Canada, cheek pressed up against perennial
creeping stems, channelling her mother's nature, enduring as intermittent
pink florets.

My mother noted its growing, shrivelling. She would pick
dead leaves, sometimes forget
water. It survived,

the care it was given. This plant. For thirty-one years, my mother
kept showing me.

SABRA, EXPLODING

Today my mother flew back to her sweltering, turbulent mother-
land, reopened the festering feud with her dead
mother. Away from bland North

American conflict with her half-
Canadian daughter, she'll fight a full-out war

with shiftless brothers her own mother loved, who never deserved
one banana that woman waved, tossed after them.

Back in her childhood
home, my mother slips into fetal position, in the garden where she was born

a hardy Sabra. Those pears she used to love
nettle her now, cause viscera to hiss, anticipating
shrapnel.

My mother doesn't worry, like me, about buses
split open. She cries, not as a mother, but like a child,
lost under headlines

in the Diaspora, for the body ejected
privately, in sections: the prickly surface breached, sweet inner flesh

embedded with bullets.

PLAGUE OF THE FIRST BORN

Ten plagues trailed me
out of Egypt, into adulthood
through stubborn history, my mother, exegeses
remembered poorly. Wherever I wandered,
like a hungry animal, these stories
dogged me.

Miracles followed. Once a year, we sat together,
all of us returned from Exodus. At Passover, we shared
a meal,[1] swore it would be the last, then served up more
grievances, each convinced she'd been a slave.

Our discord released another Nile
between us. We read curses to each other
solemnly, drowned out compassion
with ritual. We followed protocol, removing wine,
reducing pleasure,[2] the sound of forks on glass
like tiny hailstones.

Our dinner plates became battlegrounds,
ten red blemishes splattered round
the edges. Darkness settled, the adult first-
born children, full of bitter
herbs, still waited for the youngest
to ask four questions.[3] We repeated

stories, bled together sweet
wine, afflictions I can't remember.
We sang, *Maybe next year,*
in Jerusalem –

my voice a version of my mother's, irritating
the same old blisters, while, around the table,
new ones formed.

TAMAR

No Canadian 'eh' at end, or *aahhh*, when you realize *I*

didn't spell or say my own name wrong.

The native speaker's way is sticky brown, dates
cleaving tongue to roof of mouth, uvula
vibrating arrr: *Tamarrr.*

A different name, hard to say
in English. *Tamara, nice name. Where are you from?*

Before Christ. *Not nice.* Amateur harlot, sister of Amnon.
Tree. Jungle,

Jerusalem, rented house in German colony turned Swiss
embassy. My parents: Beautiful, not Polite Israeli,
and Blue-blood Son of His Right Hand.

A good family, tracing back to Queen Bathsheba's David.
My parents hoped

I would stand tall, flexible like my namesake, date palm.
I always hung,

on arc of sun, rising east, falling

left. In Hebrew letters – my name does not drag

ink. My left-hand, writing hand, won't lift
imprints of palms rereading words backwards.

My parents chose Canada, this name: Tamar.
They could have chosen Tammy, nickname *Tam*, a single Hebrew syllable
for simple.

I

written often,
say nothing

about myself.

Repeatedly.

This poem is about my mother.
This poem is about my father.
This poem is about

some trauma, having to wear my older brother's lime green
sweatpants.

I have not undressed this. I'd rather wear something
other than bareness.

I write in first person,

say nothing, often,

without interrogating

pronouns, really asking: Who
might I be?

FONTANELLE

My mother felt along fault
lines, tried to find entrance
to my thoughts, recoiled against
the hard, new mind of my own.

The first great fontanelle
had closed.

Now I had a brain
that locked, in a punk-rock skull
protected by a double cross.

Secrets stashed in hair, desires
meatier than milk or story-time.
Blushes, kisses, smokes – she thought,
who knows what else
I'd tuck into bone, never share.

ATTACHMENT THEORY

When I was one, I was born
out of my mother's back. I found memory

suspended in a fabric sack.
We used to dance, me half sleeping

while she tapped
the beat of a *bo bo bo*.

This is how I learned to speak:
the shake of her voice

from her breath, to my teeth.

When I was one, I embodied a tree,
was strong as a boulder, vast like the breeze.

When I was one, I knew just one thing:
the curve of her neck like the trunk of a tree.

I was born again from the ground
at age two, childish and clumsy and up to her knees.

Separate, bewildered, I watched while she held
my new baby sister at her breast.

NOT IN JANUARY

I thought I was pregnant because waiting
felt enormous. I was sick
always saying maybe, maybe,
yes, our house is huge

enough. I was pregnant anticipating
no period ending the sentence "should we
keep going" – And that was January,
our baby wouldn't be born
Capricorn.

I heard about cravings, I was hungry
with desperation, my belly sucked into thinking
a sour pickle was better than

nothing. I thought I was pregnant
because I was tired, all this trudging.
You said March
again, push through
this last woollen cap of winter.

Our baby was not born in April, or May,
might, not never, but not yes, ever.

I thought I was pregnant because I didn't know
what else could kick this hard
inside me.

POST-PARTUM TO-DO LIST

Flesh out blank
thank-you cards. Quell

milk leak. Open wet
paperback, thirty pages in. Wake up

inner mother. Grow
to love expanded belly. Ask mom
to water dying plants.

Google rooting
reflex, relentless crying, the get-your-body-back manual.

Translate colic. Rename sex

the birth canal. Reminders:
Losing self is normal.
So is perpetual night-
gown, circadian refusal, day sweats
drenching months.

Take medicine on empty stomach.

Keep out of direct sunlight. Do not remove the blackened remnant

of closing holes. Do not despair.

Do not panic
        if fear clots like thrush, or bloodstains form
        the name of my ex.

Follow the curdled formula trail, Rorschach coffee drips
will lead me to a better phase.

EXODUS

This is my exchange זֶה חֲזָלִיפָתִי

This is my substitute זֶה תְמוּרָתִי

This is my atonement זֶה כַּפָּרָתִי

This rooster shall go to its death זֶה הַתַּרְנְגֹל יֵלֵךְ לְמִיתָה

TABLET FRAGMENTS

 Moses discovers adultery, breaks dishes.

Shame is a ragged edge
      that grips. Something with traction,
loved, hated. That left
a hot, sticky mess, cooled. Charred, sacred.
You're not sure which, in what measure.

Shame is the remnant of anger. It sticks
      by broken ends of shattered
tablets, still pointed, dangerous as knives
in butter. Shame is fatter

than treachery
      that slaughtered the golden calf,
smashed stone into fragments you could scatter,
now lingers,

      terrifying in your hands.

‖ *After Sinai.*

I promised I'd never skip away   *a   perfect   stone.*

But then I found one, had to

test its will to dance   *above   water.*

The arguments weighed on me.

If I didn't drop something, I thought I might

drown.

I threw the tablets in, a reckless fling that missed

the real thrust: I wasn't

stone,   *would   never   be*

water.

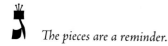 *The pieces are a reminder.*

I couldn't leave commandments where I broke them.

I packed my rucksack full of thirsty crusts,
wandered through the parchment desert,

as a fraction. I moved   *each*   *lifeless*   *fragment,*
out of honour for the body, or to bury

                                        the   *bones of evidence,*
later.

ד *Rabbi Yehoshua Ben Levi instructs us: take the broken with us.*

I gathered up the sacred stones, the tiny mass of every atom
adding up, but never reproducing
whole.

I kept the parts although they had no function for anyone, anymore

ה ו

ז
ש

ט

ל

except for me,   so I could hold them.

WHEN THE MOVING TRUCK PULLED UP

This was the final stage of love, lifting
not because he asked, but because I had to
clear the dust
under the loveseat.

Fishing through cupboards for that masala,
I broke a spice-jar, freed a pungent mix
that tripped me, opened up
a sticky-sweet corner, jammed
between dinner parties
and rickshaws.

The movers transferred vanities, heavy chests
labelled 'barbeque' and 'breakable.'
I made sure to wrap dishes, twice
or three times. He reminded me
he wanted to keep the shower curtains.

Every shelf I cleaned was full of fluff
settled in the pause
between making and takeout. The crumbs
outlined exactly what had been

removed. The dust choked me.
For a moment, we stopped, admiring

the synchronous movement of substance
rising softly, blowing up.

He coughed
before we said goodbye.

EX VIVO 1

These ex-pyjamas used to be
his oversized shirts, static
clinging to
sticky dreams. XX,
XL, now discontinued
associations: his smell,
our heat, that house, me
out of body now, threadbare
as this T-shirt memory.

EX VIVO 2

When he emailed that picture
of his perfect twins, a part of me
broke up.

Multiplied.

Our separation split between
his new life, and mine,
a little tantrum

or two. I didn't want

to be not pregnant, with
or without him, this sudden

delivery.

MEA CULPA EX PARTE

This morning everything felt elemental
inasmuch as the world shook, and I found myself still

there. After Saturday, here I was, Sunday:
carbon, water, air.

I thought I was fundamental
to his structure. I wasn't.

He didn't care when the framework imploded.

My cells were shaken, body reeling from this
stupendous culmination.

But still, I didn't scatter.

Maybe I ignored warning signs, hoping
for more. I can admit now, parts of truth

I decorated, on behalf of myself, and others: A revelation,
notwithstanding

how I saw things then.

GEOGRAPHIA

In the scraps of the longest day, I found myself:
a crossroads on no map. Erased,
where he once drew me in.

My feet, hair, skin
now separate, senseless. I found myself

in uncharted country, without streetlights,
I could hardly see my car
driving me

through lakes, computer trees
cropping up, breaking
farmland.

Before my navigation system quit,
I dreamed about his hand-
made maps. GPS could never match

that good, practical sense,
just recalculated distance
to the same foolish destination.

These thoughts pop up so rarely now –
like blue moons, memories of 7-Elevens, hopes
of winning lotteries.

The unpaved road consoles me
like a mother, rocking daughter.
I look for pointers:

the cognitive behavioural sign-post arrow,
number forty, roadkill
reminders of nature.

On the long way to nowhere, I found myself,
searching for coordinates, location
in this wild.

EULOGY FOR A GRAVEYARD AND CONVERTED CHURCH ALONG GREY COUNTY ROAD #1

I will always remember this

speck on the highway, a few tombstones,
empty can of Coke, cornerstone commemorating the year
citizens raised money.

Hustling down Grey County, on the way to the city,
I almost missed it. There is no record of how many

horses powered through this milestone, kicked gravel dust
to the shoulder.

A child's cap rests on asphalt, thrown maybe
from a moving car by a brother, while the baby was sleeping.

A monument lists twenty-five men who never returned from Europe.

An elderly couple watches us speed, from Muskoka chairs,
remembering: Days spent sowing, painting, harvesting,
meticulously re-designating brick.

They used to kiss slowly, because there was time. Their Cavalier
rusts in the driveway, now, without wheels.

He didn't want to stop, needed to get back
to Toronto. No time

for nostalgia, anymore. That couple wishes

they could stay here forever. I want to stop,
rewrite this eulogy

for a graveyard.

TWO EAGLES

My heart is two birds with clipped wings, two times
the breakneck beat of their flaps.

A clumsy craft, patched
from incomplete halves, fluttering uselessly.

Inside these birds: two hearts, and the panic
when one bird recognizes the other one, trapped.

CUSP

Like aphids on a humid day,
we staggered home together late, buzzed,
made jokes that stained our jeans
with piss and fits of laughter.

We ate berries, and sandwiches
on the swing set at his mother's. I remember

the sweet blush, trickling down his chin, how he let it
dry, while we grinned, and I could taste it
on his stubble.

By morning there was frost, a perfect layer
on my window. Had we squeezed the last drop
from summer, or was this false
spring? We left crusts

that final evening crumpled up
in foil, bit ends of strawberries
languishing on the counter.

ROAD TO WHITESHELL

This is what's left. *Shoot*

for the moon and even if you miss, you will land among
[something illegible]

says the sticker on the single pickup
I passed this hour.

I speed through *Danger:*
sharp turns ahead. Roadkill scares me more

than blunt warnings: *Risk of injury*
or death. Something tells me I am trying

my luck driving, crying wolves. I wonder if I should have
bought that lucky Lotto.

I want to return to nature, but have no idea
how to get there, without driving

wild and blind, through broken, uncharted territory.

TREMBLING ASPENS

When our relationship was almost dead, he walked us back
through that forest fire: he wanted to burn

records. The unexpected heat removed our clothes, inhibitions
wrinkled off. He begged me to wait
for pine cones

to peel open, reforest. I couldn't stand that long
on burning time and blistered feet.

Smoke had already left its stain, a black tattoo
engrained in my carbon.

All around us, surviving trees remembered
too: each trunk's concentric rings
marked fire, and rain.

We re-grew

in different directions: my legs re-rooted, his arms
made leaves.

Feeling green, we trembled together, one last time.

PROMISE TO ALGONQUIN PARK

This is my oath to trees:

     I will not pine.

     I will read between leaves.

     I will try to find moments.

This
 is a moment:

Algonquin Park, dark,
lake still, but for stars.

RECLAIMING MYSELF FROM OLD PHOTOGRAPHS

When things ended, I went crazy
with scissors, wanted no one
to keep the historical
kiss.

I found this unmarred straggler
inside an old backpack.

The date of the snapshot is
August twenty-fifth, two thousand and seven.

Both of us are smiling,
in front of Promenade Plantée.

At some point, later, I had left
that still-life, with only a carry-on.

But even this perfect picture now
seems jagged at the edges,

as if a new life could grow
from where that one was cut,

how a lizard's tail, or piece of worm
regenerates.

WHAT I LOST IN BECOMING A DOCTOR

Patience.
Patience.
Patience.
Every morning, a lot.

Shock.
Seven quarters.
Patients.

Being human.
Loose change clattering in my cranium.
Brain working for me.

Blissful ignorance.
Trust in Western medicine.
Beauty rest.

Romantic underemployment.
One hundred and sixty-four nights.

A real intense kind of giving a shit.
Disgust.
Time with loved ones.
Coffee, cafeteria eggs.

Every kind of perishable food item and indoor plant.
Two hundred pens.

Surprise.
Confidence.
Quiet.

A few minor characters I needed for the second half of my first novel.

AN AIRPORT

is a thrill that never stops. a whirring place
to meet someone, a prototype
for moving on, fast and unflappably.
it's not the propulsion of strangers, accelerated
intimacy, duty-free –
it's jet stream, magic, liberation,
wrapping iron arms in feathers,
taking off.

BODY OF NEUROSES

| What are we? | מַה אָנוּ? |
| What is our life? | מַה חַיֵּינוּ? |

THOSE THIRTY MINUTES I STOOD OUTSIDE

the Centre for Addiction and Mental Health,
muttering, cursing

under my breath, stamping
leather heels, hoping I didn't look

too comfortable. Why didn't I

wear makeup?
Maybe I should have
washed my hair, so it didn't
act so fanatical. My final medical

school rotation, psychiatry, waiting
for the other shoe to drop, wishing
I had my name badge with me.

That day, I waited forever
for you to pick me up, apologize
for being late,

and promise me I didn't belong there.

OPERATING TABLE

The opposite of invention: surgery,
a form of dividing meaning.

Take the whole of a body, expose it
in sections.

At the far end of love: assessment, separating
knee from person.

Draping hurts me, leaves a sliver of intention,
after hours lying naked, for others'
dissection.

KNEE

I glimpsed a fragment of my body
through a tear in my jeans.

My skin looked extra naked, with its outer fabric torn.

The sight inflamed me, as if I witnessed something
private.

Through a bloodied, broken window, peering in, I saw myself:
voyeur.

BITTER BERRY

Everything opened so fast, the choke-
cherries suddenly red, flesh
free of flowers, saturated
with drunken thunderstorms.

I felt my throat for the first time in a long time
swallowing. A hot, bitter memory was either
coming up or pushing down. That summer

chokecherries gushed like blood beads
from a road-rashed elbow. Someone had to
choose which fruit to ditch

and I woke up one morning still bleeding, years
past adolescence, an adult
in the grip of summer berries.

I wanted to speak, but every word sunk,
like a helium balloon filled with pebbles. My voice
burst from windpipe, jammed.

I tried to tie tourniquets, pick off pain,
clean wounds, after the injury of rain. The rusty taste
returned a flood of memory. Clusters like air sacs

inflated histories. I needed to inhale
all of them – too fast, too many,
forgetting the crux of it, filled with a tooth-
breaking stone.

AUNTIE ELINORE'S MISSING EYE

My grandmother told me
Auntie Elinore was the knockout in the family.

I only knew her with the empty socket.

I thought I had to fill something, compensate
for her misfortune when we sat together.

I made small talk while she knit, one eye open,
one eye gone. I thought but never asked her
how she lost it.

As a child, I wondered if the void would yield
like dough, if I pressed my thumb into it.
I faked, but never ate the *mandelbroit* she baked us.

Later, I practised cyclops dancing, thinking
with a nostril pinched. I'd pretend
I wasn't scared, ashamed

I couldn't see her beauty. I dreamt her sticky lashes
crawled like daddy-long-legs, drowned
inside a melted Popsicle.

I tried to focus on her good
eye. My grandmother warned me not to stare –

and I tried, but sometimes had to check if she could see–

I had a gaping hollow somewhere, too.

MEDITATION NERVOSA

There are weeks I skim along the surface

a lake-mosquito, never breaking skin. At work, at home: I flit above the probing

questions, don't wait long enough to sink.

There are weeks I cause no harm,

do no good. *Primum non*

nocere.

I make sure to keep things light, only eat for hunger.

Some days I only see reflection. The mirror,

a drain. I try not to get sucked in, but then –

I see myself, a little deeper than I am.

There are weeks I live in fear, knowing everything could shatter

with just a little taste, a morsel of weight

in the wrong   place.

IF

If:

An egg had not dropped.

        Natural disasters.

        Perpetual insecurity.

        The promotions committee.

If: I liked my mother.

        I loved myself.

        The public bus was on time.

        I could swim

                through the puddles of salty, brown water between us.

If: My skin was more coffee, or less

                buttercream.

        Artificial reproduction technologies cost less.

        I could remember what a stranger said about tacky

        cervical mucous.

If: I believed you.

        You didn't ask me.

        I wanted my career enough.

        There was no fire.

                Paradise,

      California was not incinerated.

If: I didn't drink diet, or beg for fentanyl

                after the epidural.

        I wasn't paralyzed.

        Holding my son felt natural.

        I forgot King Solomon said cut the baby

                in half.

If: I died.
           I deserved this:
                    my shedding hair, my sex life.

           I loved an ocean more than contact lenses.
           I laughed, and not ironically, writing my will.

If: I wasn't scared saying things out loud
                    might make them real.

BETWEEN THE TEMPLES, AGRA

Swaddled in the temple's clouds,
the condensed blessings of three million gods –

I am small. A puff of breath exhaled
into the universe.

Smoke that, says our guide.

Maree-wana? Opee-um? clucks the boy in the entrance, eagerly
seizing this sacred moment

for business.

Against the rooms of marble inlay,
endless petals cut in semi-precious stone,
he is tiny, dark,

a drop of ochre between the temples.

I give him nothing, but he carries off my pleasure
like a headache no pill or drug can swallow up.

BODY CENTO

from Darren Stebeleski's *Sentinel of Truth* (2012)

Dissolution, disappearance –
It's like an old basket. All it would take was a slight pressure,
my heart and stomach and a garment bag, my blood
even in the dust, sucked into the military.

Everything conceals something else:
Palm rested on the interface control –
Inner workings like a little dumb weight –
The gunnery environment –
The mouth – instead of tonsil

leathery old infections, penetration, miscegenation,
in a thousand tactical simulations.

But it makes an immigrant laugh
via some unconscious neuromuscular twitch.

It would be obscene not to.

BODY BUILDING

Your mother is not sure she likes it: you
almost unrecognizable from boyhood, your father

wonders – is this art? A reflection, maybe his own
insecurity. He thinks you have too much muscle,
the definition of omitting
Torah for gym, curly black *Payos* for lean white
meat. Every part of protein chiselled, a magnificent

Traif dinner is what you've made,
she said:

It took work to make it in this country,
with nothing. We clothed you, fed you, gave you
everything, but this body-

building is just not
Jewish.

INSIDE AND OUTSIDE

I want to forget *One is too many, No
Jews or dogs allowed.* I want only pure love
for this beautiful country: the *Noble
and Wolf v. Alley.*

I am instructed to remember
Ha'Sho'ah, miles of smoke
away, Safta Chana, Addis Ababa.
Zaydie Alex changed his name from Zelig,
on a bicycle, peddling eggs, cold
North Edmonton.

I don't want to remember
Grandma's old house on Salter Street, in Winnipeg,
toothless mother, child
sleeping by the boarded-up doorway.
Saba Shlomo never said the reason
he could never return to Alexandria

after May, 1948. And before my mother
left Israel for Canada, both my parents
asked forgiveness, in synagogue,
on Yom Kippur, the day of atonement.

I cannot forget my middle name, Sa-rah,
the name Sarai took after Hagar bore Ishmael.
My grandmother's Sheitel seemed no different
than a hijab.

I loved my mother's black mane, blue-
collar roots trying to constrict her, admired her
brown skin against white stones of the Hebrew
University in Jerusalem. And I also loved my father's blond
luck, grey eyes scanning Latin, Bloor and Spadina.
I saw myself as both:
colonized and colonizer.

When does my history start:
Air Canada, my parents
on the way to Toronto, July
nineteen eighty-four? Or Avram,
before Avraham gave up his idols?

I dance
an awkward dance, in front of four-way mirrors,
a little girl trying on big-girl
dresses in a changing room
at Hudson's Bay, Canada.

I see myself multiplied
by two and four and eight,
my parents and grandparents, and their parents
walking towards me. And in my reflection
they ask me

in English: *When will we get there?*

My body looks back from a trick mirror, I forget
if I'm *Us* or I'm *Them.*

On Yom Kippur, I ask God
for forgiveness. He asks me

to struggle, like Israel, wrestling his angel.

IMMIGRANT

You are asked to answer with an ice cube
in your mouth, full circus
chasing you, waiting to set things straight.

Between your teeth and theirs,
animal syllables, nowhere safe
for a tongue to rest. You will learn

to speak faster, make music with wire
twisted tighter. It is so easy
to trip, bite a lower lip, hard to find ground

on a scaffold that shivers. But you must
keep talking, forcing the shape of miracles,
pronouncing.

There is no translation for this.

ZAYDIE'S FEATHERS

Legend has it, he received therapy
for four or five years, before therapy was cool.
Even though therapy might have been embarrassing
for another businessman

of his stature. Accepting weakness
was his strength, even before. And after,
somehow therapy became inextricable
from an improperly recalled joke
about feathers, as they relate to baggage.

I was covered in feathers, he may or may not have said
to my mother. Freud
helped him love those feathers.

Between the life he left in Pinsk,
sick father and un-Freudable mother who tried to raise him
and his siblings in Edmonton, we know he was hauling
several feathered breasts.

> He was covered in feathers, in a manner
> only possible with a layer
> of underlying tar.

Over time, this version stuck, and history was made
inseparable from fact.

RAINFOREST (IN REAL LIFE)

How I remembered it
from Saturday visits.

A convincing imitation of the natural
history museum in Toronto.

Eight thousand
miles, three plane rides away, the same

green upon green upon green,
crickets, rotting leaves, mould
steam

streaming into amygdala. My stomach,
knotted vines, butterflies

out of my chest, through the canopy.
Maybe this is as good

as memory, preserved inside a glass
display case, every experience still
miraculous.

In the real rainforest, time stops

like stuffed birds, caught between
being and becoming old

growth. Reborn, recycled, renamed
after death.

I don't know if I want to stay (in this exhibit),
or go back

to my childhood.

MACHZOR (HIGH HOLIDAY PRAYER BOOK)

In Hebrew school, I learned Machzor
comes from the Hebrew root *to return*. But from where,

and to where, I was never told. How does one return to God,
if God is everywhere?

I read the pages dutifully, swayed from Rosh[1] to Yom[2]
Kippur,[3] my head throbbing blank

atonement. In my teens, I stole a Machzor,[4] ignored inscriptions
stamped in red ink, urging me to: *Return to Beth Tzedec.*[5]

But how to return, and to whom? Every year the stolen pages read back
my rolling eyes, sarcastic crib notes in the margins.[6]

---

1   *Rosh* (ראש): Hebrew for head; also see *Rosh Hashana* (ראש השנה): literally Head of the Year
2   *Yom* (יום): Hebrew for day; also see *Yom Kippur* (יום כפור): Day of Atonement
3   Kippur: sounds like כפרות from the root כפר meaning "to wipe out"; also, "Mercy Seat"
4   *Machzor* (מחזור): Hebrew for cycle, from root חזר: "to return"
5   Beth Tzedec (בית צדק): 1700 Bathurst Street, Toronto. Also: "House of Justice"
6   Notes in the margins: Commentary; also see: Talmud

DEATH
OBSESSION

The hen shall go to its death	זאת התרנגולת תלך למיתה
And I shall proceed	ואני אלך ואכנס
to a good, long life	לזיים טובים וארוכים

CONFESSION

I watched a man muttering, dripping

under the fumes and bustle of the butcher shop
in Chinatown.

I tried not to look. The rain hit us both

hard, without warning, like a wild dog
in the stomach. He screamed,

I killed a man, and I'd do it again!

The air was acid
on our damp bones. Pigs and calves hung

dead, upside-down beside us.

He said nothing more, and I didn't offer

my own confession.

TOOTHLESS

some people have bad teeth and good hearts.
others have bad hearts, with good teeth.
    they hang on,

with
tentative love.

bad teeth spread
premature heart disease, breaking
hearts

like a spoiled peach

Great West Life helps white ones with
Crestor. hard not to get bitter

bad clichés grow teeth:
identified by rotting
forensic entomology.

experts were taught to pronounce:

teeth.

one particularly rotten affair
caused heart attacks.

the public focused on their lack of

trying to find those people a dentist.

those are the most dangerous, because

they hide tridents

misery

and teeth.
the injustice spreads

corrupting the heap.

filling cavities
or stuck
like a wayward seed.

the prostitute with a golden heart,
dental records.

*Calliphora vomitoria, Cynomya
cadaverina.*
not easy to say when missing

almost killed her mother and sister,

compelling teeth. no point

THE DAY AFTER YOUR DEATH

For Peter Murray

Today the struggling back-
ended, yesterday
abolished tomorrow,
undid moving forward, re-

wound you to crawling,
into your parents' bed, the inverse
of birth: all hope sucked
back in, your mother's

scream contracting.

You wanted out-
accelerated after-
math, uncertainty lifted,
fast. Escape.

We wanted that.

In the end, you were like a baby,
chugging bottles of vodka
at Disney movies.

Enough, your ex-wife said, we said

nothing, or something like that.

It was hard to see
you, to love, accept
destruction. But we still did,

and didn't.

AUTOPSY

Skin, guts, bone

could not begin to describe this.
Peeling back layers only leads to more

sinew, breadth, questions of theology.

You have a body I am sure
I can stitch. But inside, a history

impossible to find or classify. My hands

tremble through each stratum, the parts I know I'd find
inside me, and the absence

of anything distinguishing.

FORESHORTENING

1. Foreshortening

Close up, she is an overripe pear: yellow, oozing
brown at pressure points.

I cannot stand looking down at her, foreshortening
expectations, telling her a circle may be
an ellipse.

2. Death Perception

This assumes we are an equal distance from the object.

3. Vanishing Point

She asked me:
>   *What will happen, you know, when I go?*

I told her:
>   *Your wrinkles will fade, the depth will seem…deeper.*

>   *Don't soften this for me,* she said.

So I answered, with all the details I knew:

>   *First, ellipses will enter your brain,*
>   *then circles will clog your veins.*
>   *Lines will erupt, like flames through dry brush –*
>   *You'll become small, and quite far away.*

LATE SUMMER

Squirrels start to bury
under leaves. Trees re-colour,
overeager fruits
lose punch.

empires

tan lines ripen into
fade.

fall

Autumn preserves
old leather-face
on rocking chair.

Summer,

once a beautiful woman
dreamt of screwing him there.

The node
shrinks
into wrinkled collapse.

between fresh buds and bald expectation
like desire

BONE CHINA

I saw the flowers: *blue rosettes.* So definite,
they would make a mama cry, clutch her chest.

I checked again, hoping a higher power
microscope would change your fate.

You remained a sad bouquet, scattered
on a thin glass plate.

Your marrow concealed
the burden no one wanted to inherit

precious, full of pain, like Grandma's
blue and white bone china.

"Blue rosettes" refers to the characteristic appearance of a group of malignant cancers under the microscope. Cancers with this characteristic appearance are more often seen in children.

STEM CELL TRANSPLANT: DAY ZERO

A gossamer, hanging on by threads, iron,
blood, navigating marrow catacombs, room by room,
bed by bed.

The morning choir tumbles in, trainees sing
soothing tact, measurements. Each resident
a stem cell

muscling bravely, rooting
for a place to grow.

PARALLEL   PROGRESS NOTES

Subjective:

10-day-old male, admitted with sepsis, meningitis.

Parents state increased agitation overnight.

New rash, possibly related to change in antibiotics yesterday.

Feeds held due to increased abdominal distension.

Almost all the places I've ever wanted to go, I've run. I'll be honest, I'm scared to waste time, or let this life pass by. I can't control much. I wish I could pray, or be braver. I am scared you can't be saved, and what might happen if you are. For now, I will document carefully.

Objective:

Temperature 38.5 (axillary), Heart rate 160, blood pressure 70/40, respiratory rate 40, oxygen saturation 92% on 0.2 litres per minute oxygen by nasal prongs.

Weight 3.5 kg (+ 15 grams).

Urine output 2.1 mL/kg/h.

Patient appears unwell, with mottled skin and bulging fontanelle.

Glascow coma score 14/15. Possible increased tone to left side.

Decreased air entry to lung bases. Peripheral intravenous line in situ. Nasogastric tube to straight drain. Abdomen slightly distended.

Ins and outs. The number of lines. Infusions through G-tubes. How many needles. Your parents' worried glances. How many times the nurses call, wake me up from dreaming. I was dreaming about my vacation in Dubrovnik.

Assessment/Plan:

1. Sepsis/meningitis: Continue current antibiotics. Will await results of culture and sensitivities.

I don't know what to do.

2. Agitation: Possibly related to pain. Analgesia around the clock.

Maybe I should hug these parents.

3. New rash: Possible drug allergy. Antihistamine as needed.

4. Abdominal distension: likely related to infection. Hold feeds and continue TPN.

Maybe I should make a bucket list.

MEDICAL DECISION–MAKING WHEN THERE IS NO BASIS FOR MEDICAL DECISION–MAKING

I'm moved by the beat of invisible
wings,

the untwisting of chains inside
my gut –
a flock of hope, my grandfather's
sinewy ghost
swarmed by grasshoppers.

I am covered in   feathers, the burden of gravity

snapping, a jackknife stab at   weighty.

I grab at depth in the break-
neck river, catch   waves, dry heaves,

not knowing.   Nothing

I can weigh   against a logical argument.

PLAYING BOGGLE IN THE HOSPICE

One

precious grain

in an hourglass up,

against three more minutes, caught

between climbing a sandstorm

and an endless

white-sand

beach.

RE:GENESIS

Sound the great shofar	תקע בשופר גדול
for our liberty	לזרותנו
And raise a banner	ושא נס
to gather our exiles	לקבץ גליותנו
And gather us together	וקבצנו יזזד
From the four corners	מארבע כנפות
of the earth	הארץ

BURNING BUSH, GHANA

Voices gush from hills,
through open windows of a Presbyterian church
nestled in the dip between two grassy peaks in Upper Volta.

The brightest lips on earth pour out
cool springs, hymns to burning refuse
in the distance.

Scenes of worship, of disposal, separated
by a few dry yards, overlap to form a single picture, when squinting
at the right angle:

Smoke in the background rises,
while close-up, wrapped heads, like new flower-buds
poke out windows, sing pink,

yellow, blue, Sunday-best...and the green! The green

never consumed.

ESCHAR

It was tough, at first,
to let you in: my adult skin, evidence
of hurt, repair, burying
evidence. The blackened bind above old burns
had long incarcerated nerve ends.

But I let you touch, again, opening
cells. The pressure liberated
loves I'd burned.

And after that, the blood
returned, through thicker skin. And words

escaped quite surely, though pinker
than I wanted.

Eschar refers to dead or necrotic tissue on the skin surface, particularly after a burn injury.

MIST AT BANFF

Mist allowed us to see
       the secret
       but constant breathing of mountains.

We didn't recognize it until
       there it was,
beaded with moisture, affirming

the presence of light.

1.19,62 (CANCER LIBRA CONJUNCTION)

For my Cancer Husband

You were the fourth sign I received
in the northern hemisphere.
I knew it by the half-bit moon, the planets
aligning, but I couldn't believe it. I asked you
to pinch me.

I met you under Saturn, a lake dispersing
spikes of honey sun. Elliptical galaxies
revealed themselves to us. Jupiter spun
cartwheels on its axis, radiating
a filigree of stars.

I always knew astrology predicted
danger: too much water, or too little
air. Your angular house, our cardinal
natures. I fell in love
with a skeleton you wore

on the outside, then shed.
You told me you didn't believe in karma.
But our karmic paths crossed again,
when both of us were irrational, searching
for horoscopes. You needed one and I needed you

in mine.

WHY WE KISSED

I.
Talking terrified us, my logic
melted in moonlight.
Before I could think, my tongue
reached. My heart
commanded it. Mixing

pistol, toothpaste.
I felt like speeding
off a cliff, a massive car
lifted from my chest.

I needed closure, opening
cavities. Possibilities: we both
needed, physical, dangerous.
Here was something:
a lip-hold to cling to.

II.
Talking   melted

Before my tongue.

I felt like closure, opening

something:

SPEAKING CROW

Sometimes I sing to you in bird, and you return
a paper clip, or shiny square of fabric.

I find old speaker wires in my hair, you transmit love
through static. Mostly, you are silent

as a syntax scrapyard. But through closed lips
I see the glint of little things

you carry to our nest: a locket or a fish bone – neither
redundant.

AEGEAN BLUE, SANTORINI

The clouds followed us down the coast,
almost into ocean foam, before leaving us
an island
halfway between seawater and a cactus blooming. Brimming
with imported water, we defied all odds,
remembered life vests.

And we also remembered stick-shift. Drove,
between dry and wet worlds, through arcosolia and loculi –
searching for permanence.

Drove with all windows open, sucking in
the pressure of salt, lifting wetness. Touched
every tight curve, our heated wheels on burning
asphalt, while earth behind us threw quips
at our departure.

The souvenir shops had everything:
almonds in honey, postcards, the replicas of
baklava or tiny churches.

Calderas jutted out
like overflowing breasts on busts of Greek gods,
declaring independence

from relentless blue. You took photos, I read out loud
Wikipedia, excerpts from Homer,
names of mountains: Emily, and Luv4Ever.

We felt like tourists, strange
to each other, suddenly. Peeling burnt skin,
we found a pinkness, newer than whites and blues,
our mythology.

CALLING WINNIPEG HOME

I entered the new number as *Winnipeg Home*
to distinguish it –

From the home formerly known as *Home*:
that closet now stuffed with high school sweat-
shirts, and a pile of lonely Valentine's Day
animals.

From *Montreal Apartment*
between Pine and Prince
Arthur, bedbugs, feeling grown up
the night the power was cut.

From the all-night sofa
of *Woodsworth College Residence*.

From *Edmonton Apartment*.

From *Home* (yet again).

From his bed, in his parents' home. From the hole in the wall
where he yanked out the cord of a rotary phone.

I entered the new number as *Winnipeg Home*,

so I could ask Siri to call, let her reassure me, finally:

"Calling...Winnipeg home."

KIDDUSH MARGIN NOTES

Let there be morning, and let there be night, ויהי ערב ויהי בקר
at the same time.

Let there be time, for a congregation of two, to count
blessings, subtract curses, keep searching re:

Genesis, the terrestrial now, a gauzy mirror ויכלו השמים והארץ וכל צבאם
reflecting celestial version: Us
candles, dancing ecstatically

through shawls, witnessing.

We set the tarnished candlesticks on our new table.

God rested, we stop fighting וישבת ביום השביעי
this particular argument,
dictated by six long precedents. מכל מלאכתו אשר עשה:

We bless pausing, the act of suspending ברוך אתה יי אלהינו מלך העולם,
creation, thank God for wine. בורא פרי הגפן

He dressed us, drew us together, באהבה וברצון הנחזילנו
undressed. The liturgy was set

such that we could modify pronouns, sing,
wholeheartedly, the chorus:

The first day of the world — זכרון למעשה בראשית,
our very first date כי הוא יום תחזלה למקראי קדש
on earth.

And after all this, we were gifted Sabbath, באהבה וברצון הנחזלתנו
resting place of chaos, old and new, this prayer
which stands for everything

again and again, and again: an opening in the Nile.

Amen.

Let us leave Egypt זכר ליציאת מצרים
again.

WEDDING CEREMONY FOR BODY PARTS

Goodnight cheeks. Goodnight neck.
Goodnight fingers, wrists, legs.

Goodnight arms, and goodnight chest. Goodnight
dry-clean-only dress.

Hello body, grown from mother's milk to stretch-
marked breasts. Welcome, weight of celebrating,

soft upper thigh and spreading flesh.
Hasta la vista, former being. Hello fears, cord

of thickened veins. Hello longing for
the discontinued beta self.

Bless you, body, like my mother
blessed new clothes, in English-Hebrew,
Honey Titchadshi. Bless me mother,

child, partner. Bless the broken bits
that make me whole.

Bless each elbow. Bless the image

of my mother, losing her accent, almost
forgetting Safta. Bless the nucleus in Yemen,

the house of brown-skinned women
in Canada.

Hello reflection. Hello perfect
imperfection. This woman is ready now,
for marriage.

Notes

Culture and sensitivities: When biologic patient samples are thought to contain infection, they are sent to a microbiology laboratory for "culture" (growing the organism on a dish) and "sensitivities" (identifying the antimicrobial agent to which that organism is most susceptible).

Sabra, exploding: Sabra is the Hebrew word for a desert cactus fruit, also known as the prickly pear. Sabra also refers to Jews born in Israel. Like native-born Israelis, the prickly pear is thick-skinned, concealing a sweeter, softer interior. The inside of the fruit is full of hard black seeds.

Plague of the first born: The tenth biblical plague was the slaying of all first-born Egyptian sons, with the sparing of the Israelites. Traditionally, the ten plagues are recalled at the annual Passover Seder (traditional dinner and ordered ceremony). While the ten plagues are enumerated, each participant dips a finger or a fork in their wine glass, and removes some wine, as a symbolic gesture to reduce one's own pleasure (in drinking wine), in acknowledgment of the Egyptians' suffering. Other Seder traditions include drinking four glasses of wine, and having the youngest member of the table ask four set questions about the Exodus story.

Tamar: The name Tamar means both palm tree, and the date fruit it produces. The character Tamar appears twice in the Torah – first, as an ancestor of King David (but only after she "tricks" her father-in-law Judah into sleeping with her) – and later, as the daughter of King David, who is raped by her half-brother Amnon. Hebrew text is written and read from right to left.

Tablet fragments: The Hebrew letters in this poem are the first ten letters of the Hebrew alphabet, and refer to the letters of the Ten Commandments. The passage in which Moses shatters the tablet fragments is the same one in which the Israelites have built and worshipped the idolatrous golden calf. *I wasn't stone, would never be water:* This refers to the story where God instructs Moses to obtain water from a stone, and disobeying, Moses strikes the stone (rather than talk to it). *Rabbi Yehoshua Ben Levi instructs us to take the broken with us.* After the tablets were shattered, the Israelites continued to carry them throughout their forty years in the desert. There are multiple interpretations of why this was done, but one of them relates to the imperative to not simply "discard" the broken (including the disabled, and the elderly).

Body building: Payos is the Hebrew word for side curls, which are worn by Orthodox men and boys. *Traif* refers to foods that are inherently unkosher.

Parallel progress notes: Rita Charon, an internist and literary scholar at Columbia University, invented the idea of the "parallel chart." In her words, these are "aspects of the care of patients that don't belong in the clinical chart but must be written somewhere."

Inside and outside: The Noble and Wolf v. Alley case is a famous 1948 Supreme Court of Canada case whereby the Court struck down a restrictive covenant that restricted ownership of land to white or Caucasian individuals. *Ha'Shoah* is the Hebrew word referring to the Holocaust. *Zaydie* is the Yiddish word for grandfather. *Saba* is the Hebrew word for grandfather. *Sheitel* is the head covering worn by married Orthodox Jewish women.

Machzor (High Holiday Prayer Book): The Machzor is a special prayer book that is read on the Jewish High Holidays (Rosh Hashanah and Yom Kippur). The literal translation of the word Machzor is "To Return." Most Jewish prayer books contain multiple detailed footnotes or margin notes on each page, which actually take up much of each page.

Kiddush Margin Notes: The Kiddush ("sanctification") is a ceremony recited over wine, before the Jewish Sabbath meal, and often takes place at home, with family. The text of the Kiddush begins with a passage from Genesis about God's creation of the world, and rest on the seventh day.

Wedding ceremony for body parts: Titchadshi (or *Titchadesh*, in the masculine) is a Hebrew word that literally means "renew yourself." In colloquial Hebrew, this is said when someone receives a gift, or has purchased something new. The implied meaning is "enjoy your something new." *Safta* is the Hebrew word for grandmother.

Thank You

To Angeline Schellenberg, for her mentorship through the Manitoba Writer's Guild Sheldon Oberman Program. To Jennifer Still, for her encouragement and for believing in my work. To Jessica Taylor, Daniel Cowper and Benjamin Rubin, who read and critiqued so many versions of these poems. To the writers in the Algonquin Square Table at Hart House. To Jordan Abel, for his generosity of spirit, and for lending a different perspective. To my editor, Clarise Foster, who made this book better by asking difficult questions and gently guiding me toward their answers.

To the medical humanities programs at University of Toronto, University of Alberta, and University of Manitoba, for working to help keep the medical journey human.

To the editors of publications in which earlier versions of some of these poems appeared, including: *Prairie Fire, CV2, Vallum Magazine, The New Quarterly, Grain Magazine, Hippocrates Medical Poetry Anthologies, The Examined Life, Hamilton Arts and Letters, Annals of Internal Medicine, Journal of American Medical Association (JAMA), Hart House Review, Canadian Medical Association Journal, Yale Journal of Medical Humanities* and *Journal of Medical Humanities*.

To my parents, Benjamin and Nava, for sending me to Jewish school, and instilling pride in my culture and collective history. To my siblings, Ori and Maya, for your unconditional love.

To the major and minor characters featured in these poems. To the broken tablets, and to the new tablets.

To my husband, Noam, and my son, Samuel – for being part of this journey, and lugging all these fragments along – you are my whole world.

Tamar Rubin is a physician, writer and mother. She has published her work in both literary and medical journals, including *Vallum*, *Prairie Fire*, *CV2*, *The New Quarterly*, *Journal of the American Medical Association*, *The Hippocrates Medical Poetry Anthology* and others. Her unpublished chapbook, "Tablet Fragments," was shortlisted in *Vallum's* 2017 chapbook contest, and her poems were long listed in *Room's* 2017 Poetry Contest and *CV2's* 2018 Young Buck Contest. Raised in Ontario, Tamar currently lives with her family in Winnipeg, the original lands of Anishinaabeg, Cree, Oji-Cree, Dakota, and Dene peoples, and the homeland of the Metis nation.